The Dentist's Garden

& Other Stories

by

Rachel Sherwood Roberts

ISBN: 1721623442
ISBN-13: 9781721623440

Hawthorne Publications

410 Hawthorne Place
Auburn, IN   46706

DEDICATED

to
James A. Roberts, D.M.D.

CONTENTS

The Dentist's Garden

When the young dentist started his practice, the windows in his operatories overlooked a patch of bare ground. He said to his wife, "Why don't we plant a garden outside the windows. That way I'll be able to see flowers, birds, and little animals."

His wife listened and then asked, "And who is going to tend to this garden?"

"I will," the dentist said.

"Well then," she said, "we'd better put in some small evergreens and a bunch of perennials."

***

The dentist and his wife planted a garden outside the rooms where he had his dental chairs. They planted mums, an evergreen tree, two shrubs, and a few marigolds. They placed a birdbath near a large rock. They build a fence around the garden.

At first the garden seemed bare, but gradually the plants grew and the flowers bloomed. While working on his patients, the dentist often glanced out at the sky.

After a time, a large neighborhood cat began to visit the garden on a regular basis. Sometimes the cat curled up by the fence and took long naps. The dentist and his patients often talked about the cat and the plants in the garden.

One spring a girl said, "There's a rabbit in your garden."

"Yes. He lives under that flowering shrub," the dentist said, and he checked to see if the little girl's teeth were healthy and clean. "If you eat carrots and vegetables like rabbits do, they'll help your teeth grow strong."

One day a grandmother with soft white hair said to the dentist, "There's a grey cat sitting in your garden."

"That's the neighborhood cat," the dentist said as he checked to see if his patient needed her front tooth crowned. "I'm always glad to see that cat visit my garden," he said, "like I'm always glad to see you!"

"I think cats are mysterious animals," the woman said.

"I think so too," Denise, his assistant, said.

***

One summer while waiting to talk with the dentist, a farmer studied the color of the plants in the garden. When the dentist came in, the farmer said, "Your plants need fertilizer, and right now they look like they need to be watered."

"You're absolutely right," the dentist said. He stopped and went outside and turned on the sprinkler. He and the farmer talked about the weather, and then the dentist

explained to the farmer that he needed a bridge in his mouth

to connect certain teeth to other teeth. He showed the farmer

some models.

"You're right," the farmer said, and he made an

appointment to have the job done.

One day a little boy sat in the dentist's chair and noticed

a little green frog near the birdbath. "I see a frog in your

garden," he said. "Sitting on that rock."

"You've got keen eyes," the dentist's assistant, Susan,

said.

"You're lucky to have seen him, " the dentist explained.

"He lives under the birdbath, "

They watched the frog then the dentist showed the boy

how to brush around and up and down each and every tooth.

"Brush your teeth carefully every day," he said, "and

don't forget to floss."

One year, when the dentist's wife came to get a tooth evaluated, the dentist pointed to a hole by the edge of the fence. "I think we have a ground hog in the garden," he said. "That's not good."

They studied the situation and decided to get the matter investigated. The dentist turned to his work, and his assistant, Sonya, took an X-ray of his wife's tooth. The dentist studied the X-ray and checked her tooth.

"We have to take care of this tooth right away."

His wife agreed and sat still while the dentist gave her a shot. While he worked, she enjoyed looking at the flowers in the garden. When he finished filling the cavity in her tooth, she said, "I think the garden is pretty."

"Like I think you're pretty," he said, and gave her a wink.

As they talked, a cat with black and white splotches

wandered into the garden and stared at them through the

window.

"He probably thinks we are mysterious," the dentist said.

The cat yawned, stretched, then sauntered away. His

wife and the assistant laughed.

***

One day a flustered woman came in and asked, "Who

takes care of that garden of yours! It's got the biggest mixture

of flowers and plants I've ever seen!"

"My wife and I do," the dentist said. Kathleen , his

hygienist, added, "Our patients give us lots of advice too."

"That's right," the dentist agreed.

"If that garden were mine," the woman snapped, "I'd put

in an all white garden!"

The dentist thought for a minute. "That would be hard to

do," he said, "because the garden is planted with flowers our patients have shared with us from their yards." He began to explain, "The retaining wall was built with rocks from a farmer's field, and the birdhouse was a gift from my staff, and…."

"Humph," the woman interrupted. "I'll bring you peony starts from *my* garden. That way at least you'll have some white peonies!"

"Then let Debbie in the front office schedule your next appointment for spring," the dentist said. "That way you'll get to see your peonies at the same time."

That very weekend, the woman brought the dentist and his wife the peony bulbs and told them exactly how to plant them.

"They'll be beautiful," the dentist said, and thanked her.

Sure enough, the next year when she came for her yearly check-up, the white peonies were dazzling.

***

The dentist and his wife watered, weeded, and tended their garden. And every year, the garden grew more lovely and interesting. The dentist and his wife shared their garden with their patients, and they gave flowers to shut-ins.

One Halloween weekend someone jumped over the fence and broke the birdbath, and one of the dentist's patients helped repair it. Another time, after a storm blew down the fence, another patient, a builder, helped put the fence back in place.

One winter as snow blanketed the garden, a tall, lanky basketball player said, "Look! There's a cardinal!"

"His nest is in that evergreen tree," the dentist said. "He likes people."

"Sort of like you," the patient replied.

The dentist grinned and explained that the retainer he'd

made for his patient had done its job. "You've got a fabulous

smile," he said. "Fabulous, like that hook-shot of yours!"

He and the young man talked about sports, and the

dentist admitted, "I wasn't very good in sports. I was in the

band instead. I played the B-flat cornet"

"But you must have done well in science too," the young

man replied.

"Well, I guess I did," the dentist said. "And, I went to

school a long time. I also worked and studied a lot."

"Was it worth it?" the patient asked.

"Absolutely," the dentist answered. "As they say, 'a

person has to do what he's good at.'"

"I've been thinking about going into dentistry," his

patient said. "What do you think?"

"When a person has a certain interest or skill, he should

develop that talent." The dentist glanced out the window at his garden. "Be honest with yourself and with others. And follow your dreams." He patted his friend on the shoulder. "You'll do fine."

***

As the years passed, children who once showed the dentist their baby teeth and who came to see him about their root canals, crowns, and bridges grew up. Patients who moved to other cities and states sometimes stopped by to see their old dentist when they came back to town.

"Does the cat still sleep in your garden?" they wanted to know.

The dentist laughed. "I always seem to have some cat or another visiting the garden. Lately a beautiful, white cat's been coming. He's pure white. Or maybe he's a she. Sandy, my assistant, named her 'Lily.'"

***

The dentist grew older. He liked his patients, and he liked listening and talking with them. He fixed their teeth, and he encouraged them.

One day after work and after his staff said goodnight, the dentist sat in his dental chair and looked out at the garden. He thought how lovely the garden would be the following spring and how beautiful it was in other seasons as well. Then he noticed a black cat with yellow eyes staring at him through the window. The cat was new to the garden.

The dentist got up and tapped on the window.

"Life is a mystery," he said to the cat. "But you and I know there is peace in the garden. We are greatly blessed."

Secret of the Rock

There was a big granite mountain where the winds blew and storms hit hard. Over time, cracks and ridges formed in the mountain, and after hundreds of years, a great boulder broke loose from its place, making a loud noise.

Animals saw the rock crashing down the hill, understood its danger, and scampered away. Such a thing was a part of their world, and they accepted it as they accepted the sun, moon, and the stars in the sky.

Now it so happened that the granite mountain was in a far away place where few people lived, so the great rock did not hit anything, not a shed, not a barn, not a house. Instead, it landed in a high flat field where wild flowers grew.

The rock felt the strength of the mountain above, but also could see wondrous things. Far below, people lived in wide fertile meadows. Smoke could be seen curling from tiny chimneys, and cattle looked like moving dots in green pastures. Straight rows of corn and beans grew in garden patches and fields.

At times the rock wished to return to its place high on the granite mountain among low hanging clouds, but after a time, the rock accepted its place and became comfortable.

***

One side of the rock was blunt and jagged, making the boulder look unbalanced and top-heavy. It seemed a mystery to people who saw it that it had not rolled over completely. The very top of the rock was flat and smooth, somewhat like a table, but one side curved upward, making a bowl-shaped area that looked like it might have cradled another rock millions of years before. When it rained, water collected in the curved-shaped basin, and birds were grateful to find water there on summer days.

Now if rocks have feelings, then one would have to admit the rock was happy, for it liked its place in the world. Once a little green lizard scurried up and around to the top of the rock to sun himself, but he soon became too hot. Another time a snake slithered around and up in order to look across the meadow, but it didn't stay long either. Birds were the happiest of creatures to enjoy the rock, but they never stayed long because their wings were always ready to lift off on fast currents of the wind.

So the rock became accustomed to short visits from various living creatures, and from each, the rock learned quiet secrets about the earth, the distant ocean, and the winds. The rock became acquainted with the changing seasons, and at night, there were wondrous stars to see and occasional

meteors that fell into the dark spaces of the valley.

One day, the rock realized he no longer could feel the tug

of the granite mountain. He had his own centre and truth.

He never wondered about his name, for he had no name.

***

During the early part of the current century, a boy came

running through the meadow with his dog, saw the huge rock,

and wondered how any rock could be so big and have such an

odd shape. He wondered what it would feel like to stand on

top of the rock. The boy became interested in the rock and

hoped someday he would be strong enough to climb to its

summit. A person couldn't just climb up there and yell, "Hey,

look! I'm king of the mountain, no siree!"

So the boy sat by the rock and thought about the

adventures he would have someday climbing the rock. And

the rock liked having the little boy in its shadow.

Almost every day thereafter the boy returned to the rock, racing through the meadow with his dog. He played around and rested by the rock, and the rock learned to like the boy, and when the boy didn't come, the rock felt anxious.

The rock forced himself to think great thoughts about the boy's desire to climb, until finally, one day, the boy turned, looked at the rock, and said in a wondering voice, "You know something, rock? Someday I'm going to climb you right to the top!"

The rock realized he could speak to the boy in the silent language of the earth.

Each time thereafter when the boy came to the rock, they talked, and their conversations were wonderful. The boy told the rock about his dog, his friends, his school, his parents, and the rock listened. The rock understood the joy in the boy's body that made him suddenly jump up and run back and forth across the meadow with his dog, for the rock also knew the tug of the earth and sky.

The rock taught the boy about the stars, wind, and the birds that flew over and stopped for water. The rock showed the boy how little ants, beetles, and butterflies liked to check out the lichens and mossy patches that grew here and there on his sides. The rock made the boy understand that it is a good and important thing to want to climb to the top of a mountain.

One day the boy said aloud, "Now that I'm ten, I am ready to climb to the top of this rock and see what the birds see."

But when he tried to climb the rock, he could not, for he was not tall enough or strong enough.

The rock knew the boy would have to discover his own

strength and purpose before he could climb to the top.

Although the boy knew parts of the rock's secret, he did not know it completely.

"When I grow older, I will know your secret," the boy once said to the rock. "Yes, someday I will know the truth."

And the rock understood.

***

As the days passed, the boy's voice changed and his blond hair grew darker. His arms and legs grew stronger. Then one year, the boy brought a girl to the rock and shared the rock with the girl. The rock was interested in the girl because she made the boy so very happy. The rock shaded the boy and the girl and wondered about the boy who would soon be a man. And the boy came often to the rock with the girl, where the two talked about their hopes and dreams. And the rock listened, full of wonder and pleasure.

***

Then one day, the young man came to the rock alone. He

beat his hands against the rock and said terrible and harsh

things. He was heart-broken and the rock could not console

him. The rock was amazed at the strength, anger, and hurt

of the man and realized the man was determined to climb the

rock.

It was rugged hard work to get to the top, and every stop

and push and pull was strenuous and exhausting, but finally

somehow the man made it to the peak. When he stood on the

top, his feelings tumbled out across the valley in a mixture of

joy and sorrow.

The rock never saw the girl again, but the man often

came alone to the rock, climbed to its top, lay in the curved

part of the rock, and stared at the sky. There was peace in the

hollow of the rock. Then one day, the man descended from

the rock and did not return.

***

The rock wondered about the man and was anxious. He missed the man with the tender heart of a boy, but no matter how often the rock questioned the wind, stars, birds, flowers and thistle seeds that floated by, there was no way to learn about his friend.

The rock tried hard to move toward the valley to search for the young man. It actually shifted in its place breaking off some corners, but it was a useless move. The rock turned its feelings inward and became cold and hard. Over time, a greenish-colored moss began to grow here and there on the rougher parts of the rock, giving it a speckled and spotted look.

Winters passed, warm springs, and long bright summer days, but the rock remained alone. Autumn came and other winters and seasons passed in between.

One day, a bird stopped for a fresh sip of water then sang a grateful song about the wonders of nature. Something about the bird's song made the rock pour its thoughts outward and upward, and the bird heard the aching of the rock and sang a song about a man in the valley who had lost his love and moved far away to forget his sorrow.

The rock was stunned and sorrowful. Why had not the young man said goodbye? How could he who once sat in his shade have left and not said goodbye? Could the bird's song be true?

The bird soon flew away.

Pelting rainstorms hit the rock, grey skies hovered over the rock, and tall grasses grew up around the base of the rock, and the rock chose to forget the man.

But the rock could not forget, for it is impossible to

forget what once had been a warm and meaningful friendship.

***

One day the rock felt the wispy end of a rainbow and was surprised with a new and certain knowledge.

"He will return," the rock said. The thought was strange and perplexing, but the idea was convincing.

"Yes, he will return," the rock repeated to the sky and knew it to be true.

***

Years passed. Then one day, the rock saw an old man come stumbling toward him through the meadow. The man was stooped and seemed unsure of things. The man seemed not to be able to see the rock for tall shrubs had grown around the base of the rock, but instinctively, the man headed for the rock. The rock then felt the man touch his side. The rock knew that touch, for he had felt those hands before.

"Here you are," the old man crooned. "Here you are where I left you."

And the rock was filled with gladness and was not bothered in the least by the old man's white hair, wrinkles, and walking cane.

"Sit on my top," the rock said. "I will cradle you."

But the man could not.

"Sit in my shade," the rock said, but the man declined.

"Then lean against me," the rock said, "and become a part of me."

The man felt around on the sides of the rock with trembling hands and discovered an edge where he could lean comfortably.

"You've changed," the man said to the rock. "You didn't have this ridge here before."

"And you've changed too," the rock said.

And so the man leaned against the rock for a long, long time and took strength from the rock.

Finally the rock said, "Tell me about your life."

The man patted the rock and spoke slowly, "You must have wondered about me. I never said goodbye. Although I have been around the world, I could never say goodbye to you. I have lived in cities, towns, and villages. I have been wealthy and I have been poor. I have seen war and violence, love and peace, but I always kept the secret of your strength in my heart."

The rock wondered about the secret. Was it the secret about purpose and character he had once tried to share with the boy? Was the secret about accepting one's truth and place? Was it knowledge about time? The rock chose not to question the man. But the man wanted to talk. The man needed to talk for oftentimes a person needs to consider and review his existence.

"I have lived a long, full life, "the man said. "I have loved and been loved, and now I have come to say farewell."

"I have been lonely without you," the rock said to the man, "for I have known you since you were a boy. How can you leave me now? How can you say goodbye?"

The man smiled. "I will tell you my secret," the man said quietly and leaned against the rock and spoke without words. And the rock understood the man.

Then the man said, "When I can no longer walk here, I will be brought here. I will become as you, part of the earth, the sky, meadow, and the whispering winds. Birds will sing to us, flowers will bloom for us, and the wide night sky will be full of golden stars for us to see, and together we will be satisfied in our place."

The old man said, "I will be back. This I promise you."

And the rock was satisfied, for he knew the man had learned and accepted the truth of all things.

High above the valley, the rock and the man leaned against each other, happy against the granite mountain, and the earth spun around and around and around the mysterious bold calling of the sun.

Maggie's Wheels

"It belonged to a little old woman who drove only on Sundays," the man said, as his wife with pencil in hand worked to get down the exact wording for their ad. He had decided to sell his mother's car, a 1976 Lincoln Continental Mark IV.

"Twenty-six thousand miles," he said. "Wait, make that 26,000 ORIGINAL miles."

The woman smiled, knowing that most people would think "the little old woman who drove her car only on Sundays" lived a plain and uneventful life, but she knew different. Many "little old women" had lived lives as grand as any. Her husband's mother Margaret, "Maggie," as she was called, was a good example. Maggie was born in 1901, and like many of her generation had lived in two worlds—one of glamour and privilege as well as one of abject poverty. The Depression changed the course of their lives. The Depression changed their dreams.

"White with lipstick red trim," the man said. "And white leather upholstery, get that in."

f***

Maggie learned to drive in 1916, "My boyfriends' cars," she said. "Tin Lizzies, they called them. No stick shifts. You pressed the pedals down."

The woman remembered that when she asked Maggie if she'd been tested for a driver's license, her mother-in-law sniffed. "People didn't have to have licenses back then. That wasn't until the 1920's. I just went into an office and wrote down my name."

"Was there a fee?"

"I don't recall any. Maybe a dollar or two."

Maggie's first adventure with wheels was in 1912, at the age of eleven. Her grandfather was one of the first in their little town in Indiana to own a car. Owner of a livery stable, he bought and sold horses. Convinced that cars were not going to be the wave of the future for the general public, he went out and purchased "two very fancy rigs." For himself, however, he bought an Overland Touring Car manufactured by Willy's Overland of Toledo, Ohio. "It was a four-door, blue, open touring car sedan with a top. No side curtains, just a top. Every woman wore a veil because it was so windy riding in a car."

Unused to such a new-fangled machine, Maggie's grand-father panicked and drove it into a ditch.

"He refused to drive again."

"What happened?"

"My parents promptly took control of the Overland," she said. "They took it for drives. They liked to see how fast it would go. I rode along."

The woman and her husband knew that Maggie's parents' speeding across dusty roads from town to town, had influenced their young daughter.

In 1927, like many Midwestern girls in search of the big time, Maggie moved to New York City. She studied piano accompaniment with Frank LaFarge, got acquainted with Broadway, played for a dance studio where well-known dancers such as Ruth Paige and Agnes DeMille rehearsed, worked in a coffee shop where she regularly sold fine Cuban cigars to William Paley, rode subways, worked at Macy's, auditioned and finally landed herself a job as an accompanist for Marie Houston, a concert singer.

For two years, she and Marie toured Florida and the East

Coast, playing concerts and meeting "famous people like the Rockefellers." Once when they were performing at Seal Harbor, "little Nelson was home from school, and I remember he went inside and made himself a cake. At one of their Open Houses, 'old John D.' gave everyone a dime. I lost mine," she said wistfully.

When asked about Franklin D. Roosevelt, she said, "I was standing on the street in New York, and he drove by. His window was down, and he was looking out. He gave me his famous grin." She said, "I voted for Roosevelt. My parents were appalled, but I couldn't help it. He charmed me."

She took her first golf lesson at "the fabulous Poland House" in Maine, and she and Marie enjoyed a room overlooking the sea at "the new Breakers in Palm Beach." During her stay, she discussed touring and compared notes with Madame Schumann-Heink and her accompanist. "Both of us," she explained proudly, "played our music from memory." She

told about the car she and Marie drove: "It was a Durant, dark-

red, four-door. We took turns driving, and no, we didn't need a

license to drive."

During the summer of 1929, Margaret married a tall, good-

looking man who "wildcatted" for oil in Oklahoma and Texas

during the boom years, then came to New York. He became a

broker and sold real estate for Pease & Elliman & Co. on

Madison Avenue. Being young and in love and in New York, the

world was their oyster.

During that rose-colored summer, Maggie's husband sold a

fancy apartment to Evangeline B. Johnson, heiress to the

Johnson & Johnson drug fortune, who "graciously invited us" to

her Connecticut home for a weekend. "At the time, Evangeline

was married to a Russian Count, having been divorced from

Conductor Leopold Stokowski of the Philadelphia Orchestra,"

Maggie said. She clucked. "It was a scandal."

So Maggie and her husband began their married life in Manhattan near Central Park and their first major acquisition was a piano.

"I went to the big Steinway store on 57th Street and played every piano in the store. Finally, I decided on 'this' one." 'This one' was her parlor grand. She stopped to recollect. "It cost us $1700.00. The day after it was delivered, the stock market crashed. Nobody had anything. By l930, everything was over."

Maggie paid ten cents for a half-pound of hamburger meat. She and her husband walked to the movies because it cost five cents to ride the subway. They took seats in the balcony for fifteen cents.

"Sometimes, after a movie, we'd buy a half-pint of ice cream for dessert," she said. "That cost us ten cents. We had an awful time paying our rent. Nobody was buying anything, much less real estate. I didn't have a job. Everything dried up. If it weren't for my brother, we'd never have made it. He had a job. He lived with us. I cooked. He helped with the rent. That's the way things were."

***

And so, like many others, their dreams died. There were no more concert tours or real estate ventures. They hung on to the apartment and the Steinway.

Expecting her first child, she returned to Indiana, to visit her parents. That was when she inadvertently drove her father's 1931 Auburn car to ruin. Speeding down US Highway 6, Maggie broke a piston ring, scoring a cylinder. "After that the car always burned too much oil," she said. Her father, a farm equipment salesman for the Butler Company, traded it in for another car.

The first car Maggie and her husband could afford was in 1932. "We bought a used 1928 Studebaker. We paid fifty dollars.

It was an iron horse.”

They traded the Studebaker for a used Plymouth, which

Maggie's husband rebuilt. “He rebuilt the engine, put in new

piston pins, piston rings, valves, fittings, rod bearings and seals—

everything. We kept it for eight years,” she said. “Then there

was World War II.”

As soldiers were called to war, they had to sell their cars, so

Maggie and her husband found a newer used Plymouth for sale

in lower Manhattan. The car featured a radio and a heater, but

“the rubber tires were so bad we didn't think we could get it

across the George Washington Bridge.”   Fortunately because he

had joined the Navy, they were able to buy tires. In that sense,

they were lucky because rubber tires were scarce and rubber

was rationed.

Maggie drove herself to New Orleans in the 1941 Plymouth,

where her husband was stationed. With her, she took her

second child, her first having died at childbirth. This child was the joy of her life and for him she played her music, "mostly classics." In earlier years, she "played all sorts of stuff for the silent films in our hometown theater. My father would come watch to see that I wasn't chewing gum."

The woman's husband's first memory of their family car was a stripped down 1947 navy blue Dodge which Maggie and her husband bought just after the war. They paid $1100.00 for it. It had no heater or radio. They put 100,000 miles on it.

Later in their lives, Maggie and her husband drove a number of different cars, including a Cadillac, a Mercury, an Old's 98, another Cadillac, and finally, her dream car, the 1976 Lincoln Continental Mark IV. By then she was a widow, once again living in Indiana. She bought the 1976 Lincoln in Montpelier, Ohio. It sported white leather upholstery with lipstick red trim. It dwarfed her, this "little old woman," who at age eighty-nine had a hip replacement, an appendectomy at ninety-one, and cataract surgery at ninety-two. She only wore glasses to play the piano and order from menu.

She was ninety-five when she explained to her ophthalmologist, "For some reason, I don't seem to need glasses to drive or play bridge."

"Writing in her chart that Maggie's vision was "20-50 plus one in her left eye and 20-40 in her right eye," her ophthalmologist looked up and grinned."You're such a fox."

She gave him a beautiful smile.

***

For more than twenty years, Maggie drove her Lincoln Continental, even as the oil embargo came, instigating a U.S. market for smaller and more economic cars. She kept her car garaged, driving it for short errands. If people commented about it, she proudly said, "My son helped me buy it." (Her son had driven her to the dealership.) She played bridge every Thursday and didn't attend church, so the woman suggested to her husband that perhaps his ad should read, "Little old woman who drives only on Thursdays." Her granddaughter drove Maggie to bridge, stiffly maneuvering the Lincoln into the parking lot. "I've never driven anything so long," she said "It's like driving a railroad car."

If people asked her age, she scoffed. "If they want to know how old I am, tell them to check my tombstone." She informed her family that when she ordered her grave marker, she asked the stonemason to chisel in the dates: Dec. 11, 1901- 19__, "but," she said, "Joe told me not to. He said I might live to the year 2000." She took his advice.

By the time she was ninety-seven she walked carefully with a cane, continued playing bridge on Thursdays, but no longer drove. "It's the *fin de siècle*," she declared.

She called her son and told him she'd decided to sell the car, but admonished him "to hold out for the top dollar. It's a collector's car, you know, a Bicentennial car, in mint condition."

Maggie's son, who had maintained the car for his mother, wasn't anxious to sell it. His memories of her at the wheel were many. This particular little old woman who "only drove on Thursdays" indeed was "a foxy lady," who, like thousands of others before the Depression, lived lives of glitz and glamour, bobbed their hair, danced the Charleston, and thought all their tomorrows would be as colorful as red lipstick and white-leather interiors.

Overhearing her parents discussing how to word and title the ad, Maggie's granddaughter leaned over her mother's shoulder and said, "It's simple. Call Grandma's car, 'Maggie's Wheels.'"

They wrote the ad and put it in the classifieds. The

following week, a man called.

"I'm a collector," he said. "I buy and sell cars, but this one's for me. I've always wanted this particular car."

Maggie would have flashed him a smile and given the sale of her "wheels" a thumbs-up.

THE END

ABOUT THE AUTHOR

Rachel Sherwood Roberts lives with her husband in
Auburn, Indiana. They and their three children remember
the wonderful cats they had the privilege and pleasure to
enjoy throughout the years: Homer, Oreo, Harry-O,
Paxton, Gratz, Alice, and Pierre.

www.ingramcontent.com/pod-product-compliance
Lightning Source LLC
Chambersburg PA
CBHW070054260726
48658CB00002B/876